HIDDEN PICTURES

I FOUND IT!

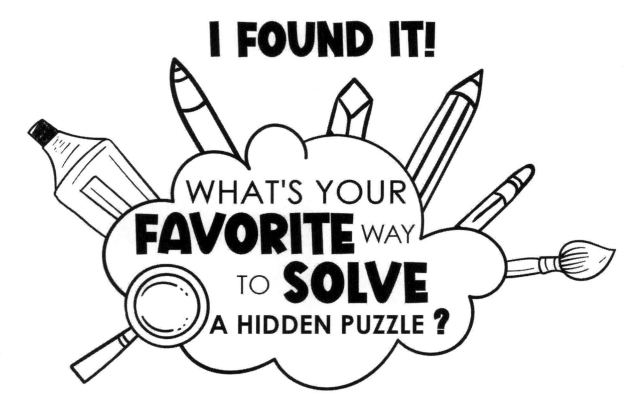

WHAT'S YOUR **FAVORITE** WAY TO **SOLVE** A HIDDEN PUZZLE **?**

There are TONS of different ways, including:

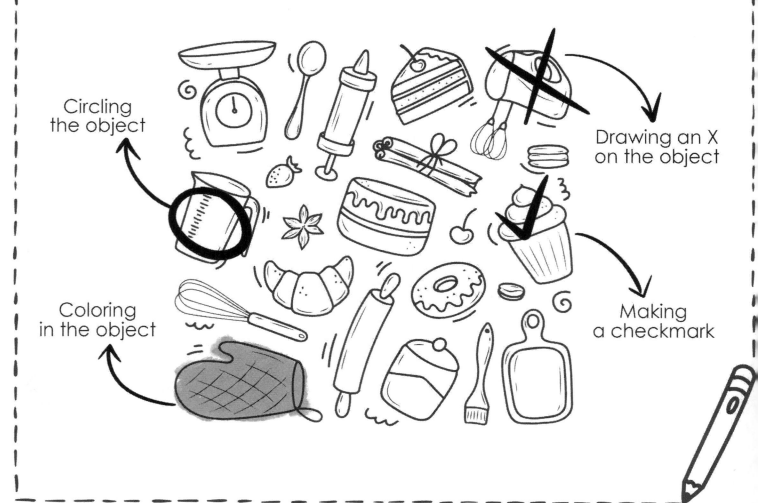

Circling the object

Drawing an X on the object

Coloring in the object

Making a checkmark

THIS BOOK BELONGS TO

....

....

....

CAN YOU FIND 8 HIDDEN OBJECTS IN THIS SCENE? **01**

CAN YOU FIND 8 HIDDEN OBJECTS IN THIS SCENE? **02**

CAN YOU FIND 8 HIDDEN OBJECTS IN THIS SCENE? **04**

CAN YOU FIND 8 HIDDEN OBJECTS IN THIS SCENE? **05**

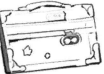

CAN YOU FIND 8 HIDDEN OBJECTS IN THIS SCENE? **06**

CAN YOU FIND 8 HIDDEN OBJECTS IN THIS SCENE? **08**

CAN YOU FIND 8 HIDDEN OBJECTS IN THIS SCENE? **09**

CAN YOU FIND 8 HIDDEN OBJECTS IN THIS SCENE? **10**

CAN YOU FIND 8 HIDDEN OBJECTS IN THIS SCENE? **11**

CAN YOU FIND 8 HIDDEN OBJECTS IN THIS SCENE? **12**

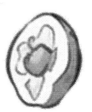

CAN YOU FIND 8 HIDDEN OBJECTS IN THIS SCENE?

14

CAN YOU FIND 8 HIDDEN OBJECTS IN THIS SCENE? **15**

CAN YOU FIND 8 HIDDEN OBJECTS IN THIS SCENE?

16

CAN YOU FIND 8 HIDDEN OBJECTS IN THIS SCENE? **17**

CAN YOU FIND 8 HIDDEN OBJECTS IN THIS SCENE? **18**

CAN YOU FIND 8 HIDDEN OBJECTS IN THIS SCENE? **19**

CAN YOU FIND 8 HIDDEN OBJECTS IN THIS SCENE? **21**

CAN YOU FIND 8 HIDDEN OBJECTS IN THIS SCENE? **24**

CAN YOU FIND 8 HIDDEN OBJECTS IN THIS SCENE? **26**

CAN YOU FIND 8 HIDDEN OBJECTS IN THIS SCENE? **27**

CAN YOU FIND 8 HIDDEN OBJECTS IN THIS SCENE? **28**

CAN YOU FIND 8 HIDDEN OBJECTS IN THIS SCENE? **29**

SOLUTIONS

LET'S CHECK IT OUT!

01

LET'S CHECK IT OUT! **02**

LET'S CHECK IT OUT!

03

LET'S CHECK IT OUT!

09

LET'S CHECK IT OUT!

10

LET'S CHECK IT OUT!

13

LET'S CHECK IT OUT!

14

LET'S CHECK IT OUT!

16

LET'S CHECK IT OUT!

17

LET'S CHECK IT OUT!

18

LET'S CHECK IT OUT!

21

LET'S CHECK IT OUT!

24